MANHOOD 101

How To Be a Man of Character and Integrity in a World of Compromise

by
Edwin Louis Cole

5th Printing

Manhood 101: How To Be a Man of Character and Integrity in a World of Compromise
ISBN #1-56292-051-0
Copyright © 1995 by Edwin Louis Cole
P.O. Box 610588
Dallas, Texas 75261

Published by Honor Books, Inc.
P.O. Box 55388
Tulsa, Oklahoma 74155

Introduction

For years, men have asked me to put the one-line statements from my men's meetings into a single collection. Well, this is it! Of the hundreds of sayings I've coined and compiled over 45 years of ministry to men, on the next few pages you'll read some favorites.

I hope they'll make you laugh, cry and think, but above all, I hope they'll help you "maximize" your manhood.

Acknowledgments

We acknowledge and thank the following people for the quotes used in this book: A.R. Bernard (24a,108b), Stephen King (37), John Wooden (108a), Bob Harrison (125), E.M. Bounds (147), and Ben Kinchlow (156).

Champions are not those who never fail; they are those who never quit.

Heroes are men who act in a moment of time on a need greater than self.

▶ ▶

▶

Some things in life are more important than life itself.

An ounce of obedience
is worth more than
a ton of prayer.

God's power is released to the degree of our obedience to Him.

▶ ▶

▶

Obedience is God's method of protection for your life.

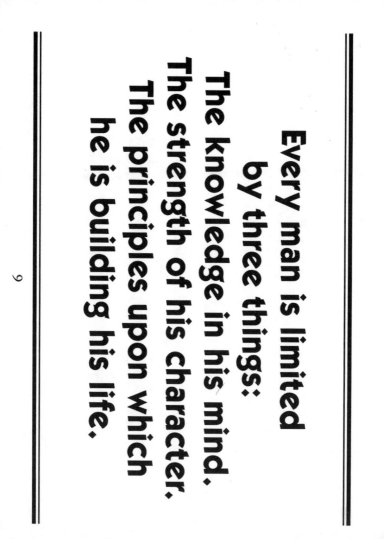

Every man is limited
by three things:
The knowledge in his mind.
The strength of his character.
The principles upon which
he is building his life.

You cannot compensate by sacrifice what you lose through disobedience.

▶ ▶ ▶

Maturity does not come with age, but begins with the acceptance of responsibility.

Every man has three
men to deal with:
The man he thinks others see.
The man he thinks he is.
The man he really is.

God, and women, desire men to have consistency, decisiveness, and strength.

▶

▶ ▶

Strength is tested by resistance to pressure.

True of marriage, friendships, character.

12

The more you build your life on principle, and the less on personality—yours or others—the straighter will be your course.

Courage is exemplified, at times, by the ability to turn and run.

▶ ▶

▶

Courage can be the virtue of the wise or the vanity of fools.

14

Men and nations are
not great by the virtue
of their wealth, but by
the wealth of their virtues.

Kindness is a virtue that attracts others to a man.

▶ ▶ ▶

The stronger a man is, the more gentle he can afford to be.

Character is more important than talent.

Faithfulness is the
cornerstone of character.

▶ ▶

▶

God commits to faithful men,
then He makes them able.

The characteristics of
the kingdom emanate from
the character of the king.

Deception leads to denial then distraction to dislocation and finally destruction.

► ► ►

If you can be deceived, you can be conquered.

All wrong conduct is based on wrong believing.

There are only three basic methods of communication: word, gesture, spirit.

▶ ▶ ▶

The art of communication is not in the ability to speak, but in the ability to hear.

Emotions follow actions.
To change your emotions, change your actions.

Life management begins
with time management.

▶ ▶ ▶

You have no second
chance to live today.

Timing is the essential ingredient in success: being the right man, at the right time, in the right place. The right sequence is vital.

The difference between men who succeed or fail is their ability to handle pressure.

▶ ▶ ▶

Perseverance will always outlast persecution.

The man without an organized system of thought will always be at the mercy of the man who has one.

The man who listens
before he talks is wise.

▶ ▶

▶

There are times when silence
is golden, others when
it is just plain yellow.

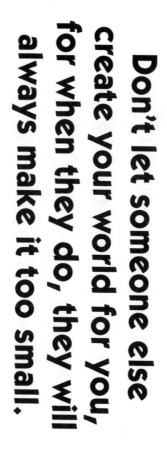

Don't let someone else
create your world for you,
for when they do, they will
always make it too small.

Pressure always magnifies.

▶ ▶ ▶

In the heat of pressure, problems loom larger; crises seem more severe.

When communication stops, abnormality sets in.

Success is the antidote to failure.

▶ ▶

▶

Success is not based on the ability to say yes, but the ability to say no.

Some people make
things happen.
Some people watch
what happens.
Some people wonder
what happened.

Crisis is normal to life.

▶ ▶

▶

Crisis is the process by which we go from transient to permanent.

Successful people recognize crisis as a time for change—from lesser to greater, smaller to bigger.

Crisis doesn't make the man; it only exposes him for what he already is.

▶ ▶ ▶

Rather than fight or flight, use crisis as a time for growth.

You don't drown by
falling in the water.
You drown by staying there.

God never quits on you;
don't you quit on God.

▶ ▶ ▶

Failing isn't the worst thing
in the world; quitting is.

True peace only comes through total victory.

God puts no limitation on faith.
Faith puts no limitation on God.

▶ ▶ ▶

It is a great thing to have
faith in God. It is greater
for God to have faith in us.

Faith is believing that
what you cannot see
will come to pass.
Fear is believing that
what you cannot see
will come to pass.

Influences that shape our lives are like icebergs: 10% visible, 90% invisible.

▶ ▶

▶

Prayer is an invisible tool which wields itself in the visible world.

Both faith and fear attract.
Faith attracts the positive.
Fear attracts the negative.

God will not do our part.
We cannot do God's part.

▶ ▶ ▶

What is submitted to grows stronger,
while what is resisted grows weaker.

Habits, good or bad, are developed or broken by submission or resistance.

We never find time;
we can only take time.

▶ ▶ ▶

Taking time is better
than spending time.
Take time now to avoid
spending time later.

Where change does not come
voluntarily from the top,
it will come involuntarily
from the bottom.

Images are more powerful
than words.

▶ ▶

▶

If you can change an image,
you can change a behavior.

When you limit yourself,
you limit God.
When you limit God,
you limit yourself.

Change is the only constant
in maturity.

▶ ▶

▶ ▶

Change is always certain
but not always good.

50

Change is not change until it is change.

As you grow and mature, your intimate friendships will change.

▶ ▶ ▶

Water always seeks its own level.

When dealing with human nature, start with nothing. For anything above that, be grateful.

People are negative by nature.

What people do not understand, they are against.

When we accept another man's philosophy, which is a rationalization for his failure, we accept his failure.

People do not do what you expect,
but what you inspect.

▶ ▶ ▶

Mediocre men want authority,
but not accountability.

Never give authority without accountability.

Men who have never failed
have never tried.

▶ ▶

▶

True joy is born out of sorrow.

You will never know the
joy of success until
you have experienced
the sorrow of failure.

Truth is life's most precious commodity.

▶ ▶

▶

Truth and reality are synonymous.

To learn you must want to be taught.

TLB

Failure is the womb of success.

Sorrow is one of life's greatest teachers.

Time is not only
measured by years,
but by inner experience.

Stress is common to life.

▶ ▶

▶

Stress is necessary to fine-tuning
life just as tension is necessary
to fine-tuning a guitar string.

Don't pray for opportunities.
Pray you'll be ready when
opportunities come.

Yesterday's dung is
tomorrow's fertilizer.

▼ ▼

▼

Take what was meant for evil,
submit it to God, and He
will change it for good.

The five greatest words in success: And it came to pass. Thank God it did not come to stay; it only came to pass.

You can gain by giving what you cannot buy with money.

▶ ▶ ▶

Men do not own what they possess; they are only stewards.

A man does not own a marriage; he is only a steward of his wife's love.

It is harder to maintain
than to obtain.

▶ ▶ ▶

Getting married is easy.
Staying married is another matter.

Marriages don't need maintenance; they need a man's time and talent used creatively to increase both value and pleasure.

71

Friendship, not romance, holds a marriage together.

▶ ▶ ▶

Giving cannot compensate for a lack of love.

You are only qualified
to lead to the degree
you are willing to serve.

You don't push string, you pull it. You don't push people, you lead them.

▶ ▶

▶

God didn't make men to be dictators, but leaders.

When your wife whispers,
"Do you love me?"
the correct answer is,
"Is the sky blue? Is water
wet? Are mountains high?
That's how much I love you!"

Good is often the enemy of best.

▶ ▶ ▶

You can have more if you don't settle for less.

God did not tell men
to be truce-makers,
but peace-makers.

Communication is the basis of life.

▶ ▶

▶

Exchange is the process of life.

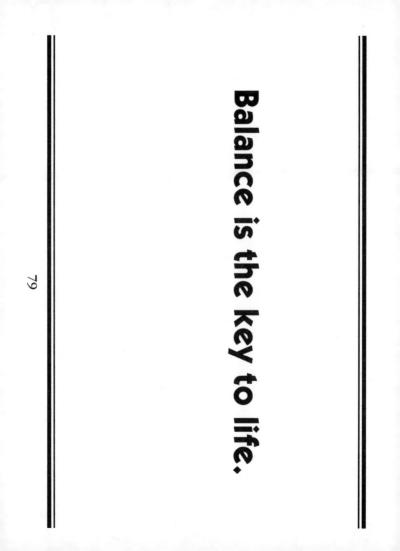

Balance is the key to life.

Agreement is the power to life.

▶ ▶
▶

Prayer produces intimacy.

You become intimate
with the one for whom you
pray, with whom you pray,
and to whom you pray.

Distance is not only measured by miles, but also by affection.

▶ ▶ ▶

A man may give his wife a mink coat, but a good name is his best gift.

The absence of confession denotes absence of commitment. Living together is involvement; being married is commitment.

You are committed
to what you confess.

▶

▶ ▶

Giving your family your
time shows respect for them.

When the charm wears off, there is nothing but character left.

You cannot know God by explanation, only by revelation.

▶ ▶ ▶

A father's responsibility is not to make his child's decisions, but to let the child watch him make his.

Fathers who punish children
for doing wrong, when
they haven't first taught
them how to do right,
are themselves wrong.

God never builds on a negative;
He always builds on a positive.

▶ ▶

God never ends anything
on a negative; He always
ends on a positive.

Children will not always
listen to you, but they
will always imitate you.

A trust fund is no substitute
for a fund of trust.

▶ ▶ ▶

To change your life,
change your words.

Knowledge is the acquiring of facts. Understanding is the interpreting of facts. Wisdom is the application of facts.

We tend to judge others by their actions, ourselves by our intentions.

▶ ▶ ▶

You qualify for having your own by being faithful in that which is another man's.

A reason some men fail
and others succeed is
their attention to detail.

Musicians use timing to
make a symphony. Families
use time to make harmony.

▶
▶ ▶

Reward in public.
Punish in private.

New construction is always easier than reconstruction.

Agreement is the place of power.

▶ ▶ ▶

Agreement produces power; disagreement results in powerlessness.

To talk to his children about God, a man needs to first talk to God about his children.

Hearing from God doesn't depend on age. It depends on relationship.

▶
▶ ▶

Peace is the umpire for knowing the will of God.

Passion is the sin of youth.
Pride is the sin of middle age.
Prejudice is the sin
of old age.

Dreams are the substance
of every great achievement.

▶ ▶ ▶

God-given dreams in God-favored
men make a God-blessed world.

Personnel is always
the problem. Personnel
is always the solution.

We are motivated to become what we imagine ourselves to be.

▶ ▶ ▶

God created man in His image. Men spend their lifetimes trying to return the favor.

Expectancy is the atmosphere for miracles.

Above the clouds,
the sun always shines.

▶ ▶ ▶

God never explains Himself;
He only reveals Himself.

Enthusiasm is an emotion.
Optimism is an attitude.
Faith is a substance.

Worry is a substitute for prayer.

▶ ▶ ▶

Worry centers on self;
prayer centers on God.

God's love is unconditional.
God's promises are
conditional. Man's error
is transposing them.

Failure to prepare is preparation for failure.

Preferences are negotiable.
Convictions are non-negotiable.

Responsibility for success depends on the willingness to be responsible for failure.

Fame can come in a moment, but greatness comes with longevity.

▶
▶ ▶

Gentleness is a virtue of the strong, not a vice of the weak.

Your care for others is the measure of your greatness.

TLB

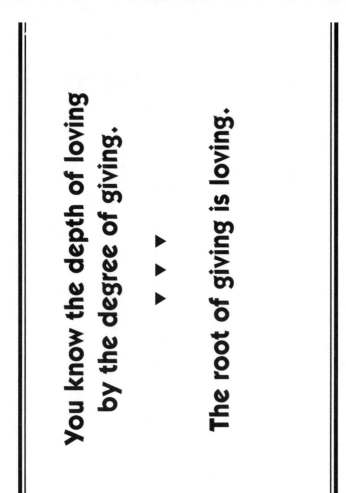

You know the depth of loving
by the degree of giving.

▶ ▶ ▶

The root of giving is loving.

112

Our relationships with others
are reflections of our
relationship with God.

There is a high cost for low living.

▶ ▶

▶

Common courtesy prevails
in peaceful homes.

Tell your wife every day
that she is God's gift
to you, and you love her.

115

To love someone is to work for their highest good.

▶ ▶

▶

Listening is a virtue of loving.

The greatest thing
a father can do for his
children is love their mother.

Love desires to benefit others even at the expense of self because love desires to give.

▶ ▶
▶

Lust desires to benefit self even at the expense of others because lust desires to get.

Lust is insatiable.
Love is easily satisfied.

The only reason you do wrong is because you don't do right.

▶ ▶ ▶

The quality of the product depends on the quality of the materials used.

The cheaper the merchandise, the higher the gloss. True of furniture, knives, people.

More than one man has dug his grave with his teeth.

▶ ▶ ▶

In the parable of the talents, the man who did the least talked the most.

Men go to heaven based
on what they do, not based
on what they don't do.
Men go to hell based
on what they don't do,
not based on what they do.

123

Procrastination steals time, kills initiative and destroys production.

▼ ▼ ▼

Personal philosophy determines public performance.

124

The man who knows how
will always have a job.
The man who knows why
will always be his boss.

Influence is one of life's most valuable commodities.

It is wisdom to apply it, criminal to sell it.

▶ ▶

▶

You can get a man to do almost anything if you'll listen to him long enough.

126

Listening is the art
of communication.
Shown in leadership,
counseling, salesmanship,
and marriage.

Success and happiness are by-products, not goals.

▶ ▶

▶

You don't make a success in life by concentrating on your weaknesses, but by going to your strengths.

One of the most powerful things you can do in life is to create an image.

The next most powerful is to destroy it.

A broken promise, to a child,
is the same as a lie.

▶ ▼ ▶

A half-truth is a whole lie.

The reward of the trustworthy is more trust.

Trust is extended to the
limit of truth, and no more.

▼ ▼ ▼

Truth may be hard to swallow,
but most medicines are.

To trust in what is short
of or beyond truth is
to trust in a lie.

Private renunciation of sin precedes public denunciation of sin.

▶ ▶ ▶

Man whitewashes.
God washes white.

A man who honors God privately will show it with good decisions publicly.

Wisdom gives men a long good life, honor, pleasure, and peace.

TLB

▶ ▶

▶

God's patterns for victory are: wisdom, strategy, victory.

Men want victory.

God gives strategy.

God is a miracle worker, not a magician.

Once you make a choice, you become a servant to that choice.

▶ ▶ ▶

The freedom of choice is the only true freedom we have.

People are not paid for
what they intend to do,
but for what they do.

Impatience is the tool of the flesh. Misunderstanding is the tool of the devil.

▶ ▶ ▶

Master your passion or your passion will master you.

140

Huge disagreements escalate from small misunderstandings.

You cannot mold clay when it is dry.

▶ ▶ ▶

It takes more humility to receive
than it does to believe.

Receiving is as important as believing.

Not all of passion is love
and not all of love is passion.

▶ ▶ ▶

A man's word is the measure
of his character.

Bring your word to the measure of your manhood and your manhood to the measure of your word.

What you believe about God has the greatest potential for good or harm in your life.

▶ ▶ ▶

Everything God does is according to a pattern and based on a principle of His Kingdom.

146

God's methods are men.
While men look for better
methods, God looks
for better men.

You can tell the nature of a man
by the words he chooses.

▶ ▶

▶

You can tell the character of
a man by the friends he keeps.

Illusions of grandeur are
not visions of greatness.

Where you are today is the result of your choices yesterday.

▶ ▶

▶

Life is composed of our choices and constructed by our words.

The true test of character is
not in what you do in public,
but in what you think
when you're all alone.

Leaders determine to influence.
Followers only happen to influence.

▶ ▶

▶

Men can make an impression
or an impact.

The man is more
than the message.
You believe in the message.
because you believe
in the man.

The more your build your life on truth, the better will be your way and the greater will be your life.

▶ ▶

▶ ▶

Truth is like soap—it's no good unless it's applied.

Manhood and Christlikeness are synonymous.

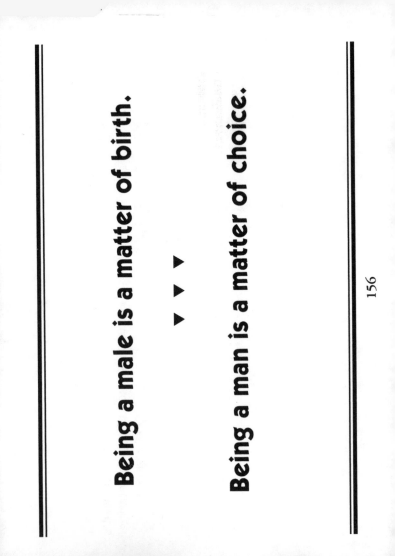

Being a male is a matter of birth.

▶ ▶ ▶

Being a man is a matter of choice.

156

Edwin Louis Cole, founder and president of the Christian Men's Network, speaks with a prophetic voice to the men of this generation. His message that "Manhood and Christlikeness are synonymous" declares a standard for manhood that has impacted millions of lives. He is an internationally acclaimed speaker, television personality, best-selling author and motivational lecturer. Cole travels extensively, showing men how to realize their dream of real manhood by looking to Jesus Christ as their role model.

Other titles by Edwin Louis Cole include:

Communication, Sex and Money
Courage: A Book for Champions
Entering and Leaving Crisis and Change
Facing the Challenge of Crisis and Change
Maximized Manhood
The Glory of Sex
The Unique Woman
(Co-authored by Nancy Cole)

To receive Edwin Louis Cole's
publication *Courage*, write:

Edwin Louis Cole Ministries
P.O. Box 610588
Dallas, Texas 75261

Dear Reader:

If you would like to share with us a couple of your favorite quotes or ideas on the subject of *manhood*, we'd love to hear from you. Our address is:

Honor Books
P.O. Box 55388, Dept. J.
Tulsa, Oklahoma 74155

Additional copies of this book and other portable book titles from **HONOR BOOKS** are available at your local bookstore.

P.O. Box 55388
Tulsa, Oklahoma 74155